WHY DO BUGS BITE AND STING?

This edition is published by Armadillo, an imprint of Anness Publishing Ltd,
108 Great Russell Street, London WC1B 3NA; info@anness.com

www.annesspublishing.com; twitter: @Anness_Books

If you like the images in this book and would like to investigate using them
for publishing, promotions or advertising, please visit our website
www.practicalpictures.com for more information.

A CIP catalogue record for this book is available from the British Library.

Publisher: Joanna Lorenz
Designed by Helen James

PUBLISHER'S NOTE
The author and publishers have made every effort to ensure that this book
is safe for its intended use, and cannot accept any legal responsibility
or liability for any harm or injury arising from misuse.

Manufacturer: Anness Publishing Ltd,
108 Great Russell Street, London WC1B 3NA, England
For Product Tracking go to: www.annesspublishing.com/tracking
Batch: 7190-23392-1127

WHY DO BUGS BITE AND STING?

And other questions and answers about creepy crawlies

WRITTEN BY STEVE PARKER • ILLUSTRATED BY GRAHAM ROSEWARNE

ARMADILLO

Introduction

Bug, creepy crawly, mini-beast, pest – these are names we use for all sorts of small creatures including beetles, flies and other insects, spiders, scorpions and other arachnids, snails, slugs and other molluscs, centipedes and millipedes, leeches, earthworms, roundworms, flatworms… The list goes on and on and on. What all these creatures have in common is that they are invertebrates – animals without backbones.

These animals have something else in common – many people don't like them or are actually frightened by them. And it is true that some bugs are pests. They destroy our garden plants and farm crops. They live on our pets, farm animals and even on us! Some spread dirt and disease.

Some creepy crawlies can also bite and sting. But it's nothing personal. Bugs are just trying to survive, like all other animals. This book shows their fascinating world, and will help you to understand how they live their tiny lives.

Contents

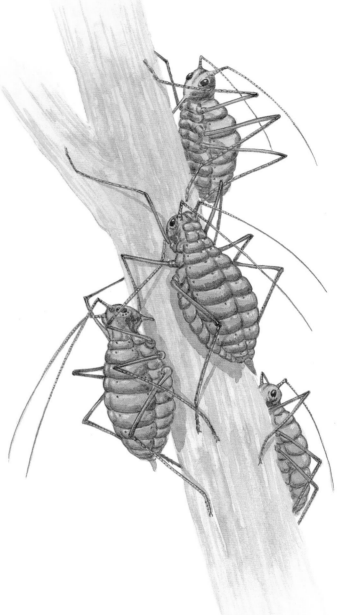

Bite and sting?

Is it just to annoy you or even hurt you? No, not really. Bugs go about their business, looking for food and nesting places, and trying to breed. If an animal tries to stop them or harm them, then they fight back, using whatever means they can. Some bugs have powerful venoms to make up for their tiny size. They sting or bite when they think that their lives are in danger, perhaps from a gigantic creature, such as you, who is about to kill them. Of course, some bugs bite because you are their food – or they think you are!

The **green scorpion** is a fast runner, and the sharp sting at the end of its tail can inject venom. This bug uses venom mainly for self-defence or to stop its prey from struggling. Scorpions sometimes come into houses to feed on the insects attracted by food or the house lights. So if you are in South America it's always wise to check before you sit down – in case there is a green scorpion lurking!

When a bee, such as these **bumblebees**, stings you, that's the last thing it will ever do. The sting's backward-pointing barb sticks in the victim. The whole sting and venom bag are ripped from the rear of the bee's body, and the bee soon dies. But the sacrifice is worthwhile to protect the rest of the bee's nest against intruders. These bumblebees are ready to defend their nest, but the mouse quickly runs away.

6

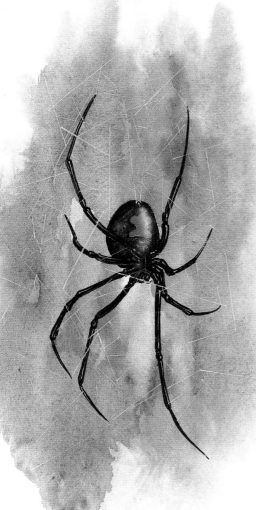

If you ever see this creature, get out of the way at once! It's a **black widow spider**. It may be small, but its venomous bite can be deadly. However, its venom is used mainly to kill its insect food. The spider jabs its fangs into a victim and injects the venom. Its prey is soon still and quiet. Its insides get dissolved while it's still alive by the juices from the bite!

By the time you feel a **mosquito** on your skin, it is already drinking your blood, which is its food. This insect's mouth is like a sharp-tipped drinking straw. It slides its mouthparts through the top layer of your skin. The mosquito's saliva stops your blood from clotting as it bites and sucks. This saliva also causes the itchy red spot you get afterwards.

Huge, antler-shaped jaws give the **stag beetle** its name. It looks as if these beetles could give you a nasty bite. But the jaws are so heavy, and the muscles that move them are so weak, that the beetle can hardly bite at all. The jaws are for show and for battling with other males. The male stag beetles grapple and push each other to impress females.

7

Look so bright?

Because it's the latest fashion? No!
To get noticed? Yes. Sometimes some
bugs want to attract a partner for mating.
Their wings, bodies and other body parts
are as bright as possible. This makes
them stand out from dull environments,
so their mates can see them easily.
Other bugs are bright as a warning.
They may have stings or venoms to
defend themselves, or their bodies
might taste horrible. Their patterns
and markings mean: 'Stay away!
I am dangerous!' Other bugs
are bright to blend in with
their vivid surroundings.

Many bugs, such as the **red-spotted
ladybird or ladybug**, use their strong
markings to warn others that their
flesh tastes foul. A young
predator, such as a bird,
might try to eat one. It soon
learns that the meal
tastes horrible. So it
avoids similar animals in the
future. A few ladybirds may
get eaten, but others are saved.

A bright animal like the **African devil mantis** would
show up against a dark background, such as brown
bark. But among the brilliant tropical flowers it is hardly
noticed. The mantis blends in among the blooms. Its
shape helps, too. Its head, body and legs look like
petals and stems. When an animal blends in with the
background like this, it is called camouflage. The mantis
is a fierce hunter. Other insects do not see it hiding
among the petals. As its prey wanders past, the mantis
grabs the insect in its spiny front legs. The mantis is a
cunningly camouflaged carnivore!

What's this – another wasp warning of its sting? No, this **hoverfly** (below) is totally harmless. It differs from a wasp in the way it flies. The hover fly darts to and fro, backwards and sideways, and hovers in mid air like a tiny helicopter. But many animals are fooled by its yellow-and-black stripes and leave the hoverfly alone. Copying hues and patterns like this is called mimicry. The hover fly is a harmless mimic of the wasp.

Would you touch this yellow-and-black insect? Hopefully not, because you might get stung! Other animals also avoid the **common wasp** (above) for the same reason. Its bold stripes show up clearly and warn you about the sharp sting in its tail. If you leave it alone, the wasp will probably cause no harm. After feeding on sweet or sugary foods, it should buzz off back to its nest.

It is dim and gloomy in the middle of a tropical forest. Little sunlight gets through the thick layers of leaves, twigs and blossom far above. But here and there shafts of sunlight shine into a clearing. **Blue morpho butterflies** flit and dance in the rays. Their brilliant wings glow and glitter. They are showing off to other blue morphos. It's their courtship flight, to attract partners for breeding.

9

Stay so small?

There are lots of reasons. The bodies of many bugs have a hard, strong outer casing. It is like a skeleton on the outside. This protects and supports the animal. If bugs grew too big, the casing would become too heavy to move or it may even crack! Another reason is that bugs breathe through air tubes. These go from the surface of the body to the inside. If the tubes were too long, bugs would not get air quickly enough into their body and they would suffocate! Also, large animals have to find much more food, which can be difficult and dangerous. Bugs' answer is to stay small!

The **fairy fly wasp**, one of the tiniest insects, looks like a fly. This wasp is so small that it would fit inside this 'o'. It can hide from its enemies in the tiniest crack or crevice. But smallness has its problems, too. You can't fight back against predators, as they are all bigger than you!

What's that small cloud flickering among the trees on a warm summer's evening? It is a swarm of **midges**. Thousands of them flit and fly together, dancing and courting and mating in mid air. Midges are types of tiny flies. Some feed on plant juices. Others bite animals, including people, and suck their blood and body fluids. The bite leaves a small, red, itchy spot. Midges stay small because it means they can move around easily to find food.

10

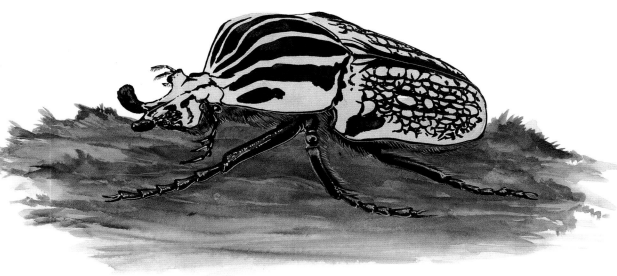

The **Goliath beetle** is about as big as a bug can grow – it can reach a length of 11cm/4¼in. If it were any larger, the Goliath beetle wouldn't be able to move at all. Its outer casing is very thick. This means the beetle is heavier than any other insect, more than 90g/3½oz. So the Goliath beetle cannot run fast. But its thick casing is good protection against its enemies in the tropical forests of Africa.

Although **mites** are very small, they have a big effect on the lives of plants and animals. Mites are found almost everywhere. They are arachnids, as you can tell from their tiny eight legs. There are thousands of kinds of mites. Some pierce plants to suck sap. Some bite animals to drink blood. These red mites are hitch-hiking a ride on a spider's leg!

The **elephant hawk moth** is the jumbo jet of the insect world. Its wings are about 7.5cm/3in across. Like all moths and butterflies, it hatches from its egg as a caterpillar. As caterpillars grow, they shed their skin. The skin underneath needs time to harden. If they were any bigger, the casing might bend or crack before it could harden.

WHY DO BUGS...

Have lots of legs?

To run fast? Yes, sometimes. Some bugs, such as the millipede, have hundreds of legs but move very slowly. For other bugs, having lots of legs gets them out of all sorts of trouble – they can run or jump away from enemies with ease. Various types of bug bodies and legs have evolved over millions of years to suit different environments. Insects have six legs. Spiders, scorpions and other arachnids have eight. Centipedes and millipedes have dozens. Some bugs, such as worms, don't have any legs at all!

All insects have six legs, but these are not always the same in shape or size. Legs are not always used in the same way, either. Crickets and grasshoppers, such as the **creosote bush grasshopper**, have long, strong back legs. They use them to leap high and far, to escape from danger. The legs have other interesting uses, too. By rubbing them on other body parts, some grasshoppers and crickets make their chirping song.

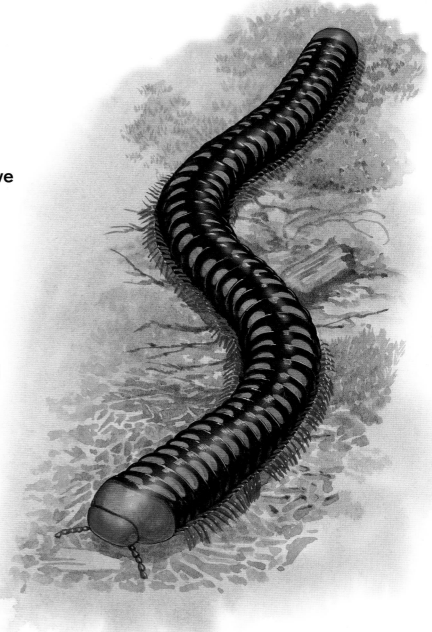

The name *millipede* means 'thousand-legged'. But even this **giant millipede** does not have 1,000 legs. Most millipedes have between 100 and 300 legs. Each leg moves back and then forward, slightly after the leg in front. This shows as a wave-like pattern moving along the side of the body. A millipede seems to glide along, as though on lots of tiny wheels.

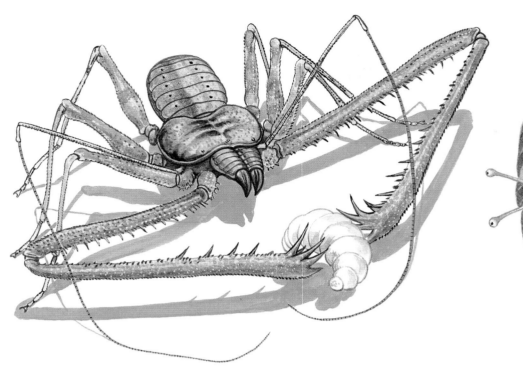

The **tailless whip scorpion** has eight legs, just as other scorpions do. But it uses only six for walking. The front pair are much longer and thinner. They are feelers, used for finding the way by touch. The whip scorpion also has two huge, long and powerful pincers in front of the feeler legs. These pincers are used to grab its prey.

Many **great black slugs** are black. But some are other shades, even yellow! Slugs and snails are molluscs. They do not have legs, but they do have a foot. This is the flat, sticky base of the body. The slug slides along by tiny, wave-like ripples of the muscles in its foot. It sticks to smooth ground surfaces by producing a liquid called mucus. This slime is left behind as a shiny trail.

The **cave centipede** runs swiftly on its long, thin legs. It also uses them to feel its surroundings, as it cannot see in the cave's blackness. Centipedes are fast, fearsome hunters of tiny animals. They have two legs on each segment, or body section. Millipedes are slower. They eat plants and rotting foods, and they have four legs on each body segment.

Need wings?

For flying! All bugs with wings are insects – moths, flies, beetles and so on. Most insects have two or four wings. They flap them to fly. But why fly? This way of getting about has some good points for small creatures such as insects. They can escape quickly from predators that live on the ground. (Although they might meet an aerial hunter, such as a bird, bat or other insect.) Also, flying is far faster than walking or running. This is important when you only have a short time to find food, a place to nest and a mate.

Wing case

Flight wing

The **green lacewing** flies in search of prey. It feeds mainly on aphids, which damage garden plants and farm crops. The 'laces' in its wings are veins, strong tubes that carry insect blood. Some of the veins are hollow and pick up the vibrations made by shrill bat squeaks. This helps the lacewing to avoid getting caught.

The **cockchafer** is a big, strong beetle. Like other beetles, it has two pairs of wings. Well, the first pair are not really wings. They are tough, hard, curved wing cases that form the beetle's 'back'. They protect the second pair of wings, which are folded up underneath them. These flight wings are thin and delicate, like normal insect wings. To fly, the beetle holds up the first pair, and unfolds and flaps the second pair.

14

The biggest wings in the insect world belong to the rare **Queen Alexandra birdwing butterfly**. This bug has a wing-span of about 25cm/10in and lives in tropical forests in South-east Asia. Butterflies and moths have four wings. On each side, the two wings are linked by tiny hooks, so they beat together. The wings themselves are almost transparent. But they are covered with thousands of tiny scales, which give them their beautiful tones and patterns.

Flies, such as this **cranefly**, make up a huge group of insects. A fly has only two wings, not four like most insects. This bug group includes houseflies, horseflies, botflies, blowflies, dungflies, fruitflies, mosquitoes, gnats, midges and thousands of others. The cranefly is a large fly with long, spindly legs. The legs hang below its body as it flies along, slowly and clumsily.

A few insects, such as this **silverfish**, have no wings. They include springtails, bristletails and firebrats, as well as silverfish. They are mostly very small, live in soil and often move about at night. The silverfish lives in houses. It feeds on scraps of food and anything else it can eat – even the glue or paste that holds wallpaper on the wall!

15

Have more than two eyes?

Not all bugs have more than two eyes. The number and type of eyes a bug has depends on its lifestyle and the environment in which it lives. Most insects are 'bug-eyed'. They have two big eyes, one on each side of the head. You only have one lens in each eye, but these 'bug eyes' are made up of lots of tiny lenses. Some bugs have extra eyes, which are smaller and simpler than the main ones. These eyes are often on the top of the head. There are also bugs that have no eyes at all. They live in caves, in the soil or in the water, where there is little or no light. They don't need eyes to see in the dark!

This **zebra jumping spider** is looking at you! Its main pair of eyes are big and shiny. There are also three pairs of smaller eyes on the sides of its head. These can see things moving nearby, such as small insects. Once it has spotted the prey, the spider turns to face it and takes a good look with its main eyes. It judges how far away the victim is – and then jumps in for the kill.

Would you like eyes on stalks that wave around your head, and then pull back into your face for safety? The **giant African land snail** has an eye at the tip of each head tentacle, which do exactly this. But these eyes can't see details. They pick out only blurred patches of light and dark. That's enough for the snail to find its food, which includes both farm crops and dead animals – they even eat other snails! This fist-sized mollusc has become a pest in many warmer parts of the world because of its fondness for farm crops.

16

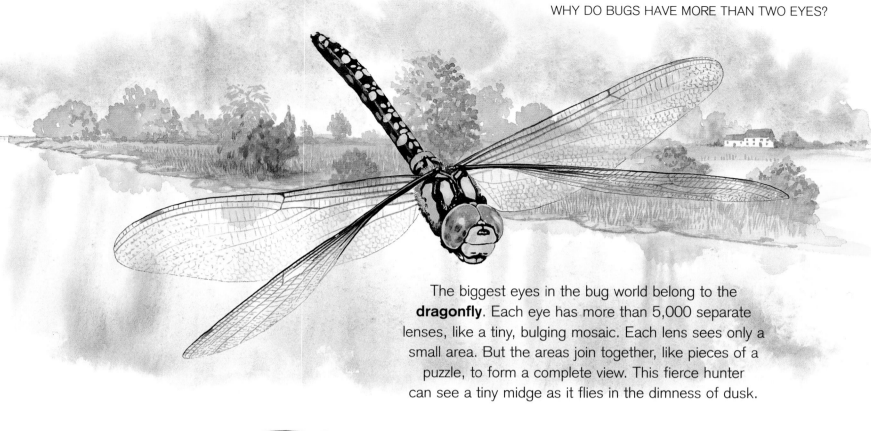

The biggest eyes in the bug world belong to the **dragonfly**. Each eye has more than 5,000 separate lenses, like a tiny, bulging mosaic. Each lens sees only a small area. But the areas join together, like pieces of a puzzle, to form a complete view. This fierce hunter can see a tiny midge as it flies in the dimness of dusk.

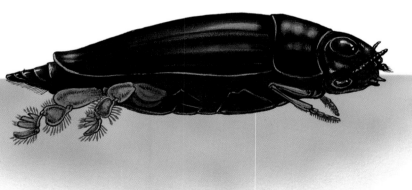

Proper eyes aren't much use in the darkness of the soil, so earthworms don't have them. But they do have light-detecting patches of skin, especially on the upper part of the head, to warn when they get too near the surface. The **giant Australian earthworm** is no ordinary worm. It grows 4m/13ft long, is thicker than a thumb and squirts a horrible-smelling liquid at its enemies!

If you open your eyes underwater things look blurred. Our eyes are designed for seeing in air. The **whirligig beetle** does not have that problem. This tiny beetle swims and whirls rapidly in circles on the surface of a pond. Both its eyes are divided into two parts. The top half looks up into the air. The bottom half looks down into the water.

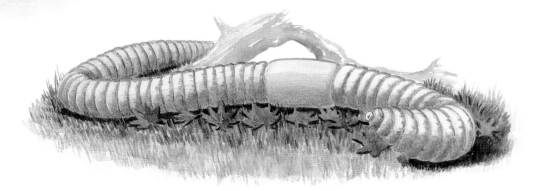

Have no teeth?

Yes, it's true. Bugs do not have teeth. That is, they don't have true teeth, like the teeth belonging to humans, cats, dogs, snakes and some fish. Of course, bugs have mouths for eating and drinking. And the mouths have various parts for getting the food into the body. These parts are simply called mouthparts. The way a bug's mouthparts look and work depends on how the bug feeds. Some bug mouthparts are shaped like fangs, spears, daggers or pincers. Others are like needles, suckers, sponges or even drinking straws.

Proboscis coiled for flying

Proboscis uncoiled for feeding

If you drink a thick milkshake through a hollow straw, you have to suck hard. Butterflies, such as this **red admiral**, and moths do the same. Of course, they don't usually drink milkshakes! They sip and suck a thick, sweet liquid, called nectar, from flowers. A butterfly's mouthparts are shaped like a drinking straw and are called a proboscis. When the butterfly is not feeding, the proboscis is coiled up under the head.

All spiders have two sharp and fearsome fangs to kill their victims. The **trapdoor spider** has very large fangs. The fangs are black and shiny and are on the front of the spider's head. Its tiny mouth is just behind the fangs. Each fang is fixed to a short, furry part of the mouth, which has a hole through it leading to the fang. The spider jabs the fangs into its prey, and injects venom through the holes and fangs. Few creatures escape the fangs of death!

Fangs

If you spill a drink or some juicy food, you might mop it up with a sponge. This is how flies, such as the **bluebottle**, feed. Their mouthparts are shaped like a sponge-on-a-stalk. First the fly oozes digestive juices from its mouth on to the food. This makes the food runny and watery, like soup. Then the fly dabs its spongy mouthparts on to the soupy food and mops it up.

Your teeth and jaws would soon wear away if you ate nothing but solid wood. Yet that is what the **death watch beetle** eats. Its mouthparts are like strong pincers that move from side to side on powerful jaws. The beetle chews, bores and tunnels its way through the solid wood and emerges from a small hole. At breeding time the beetle taps its jaws on the wood to attract a mate.

Sap is the 'blood' of a plant. It flows through tubes inside the stems, stalks and leaves. It is sweet and full of nutrients and goodness – excellent food! Many bugs, such as these **aphids**, have a sap-sucking way of life. The mouthparts of an aphid are shaped like a tiny, hollow dagger. The aphid jabs them through the plant's outer layer into a sap-carrying tube, and drinks its fill.

19

Lay many eggs?

Human parents usually have one or a few children, rarely more than ten. Bugs are very different. They produce hundreds, thousands or even millions of offspring! Most female bugs lay eggs, which the young hatch from. Why do they lay so many? Most bugs, especially insects, are small and juicy. They are food for frogs, lizards, birds and many other animals. The more young that bugs produce, the more chance that a few of them will not get eaten. The survivors grow up to have their own babies, and carry on their kind. It's survival by numbers!

Queen termite

Worker termites

King termite

Inside the hard, heat-baked mud walls of the termite tower is the 'Termite Royal Palace'. The **queen termite** lives here, lays eggs here – and does nothing else. She is the only termite in the nest to produce young. Her body is a huge, swollen, egg-laying factory. Her breeding partner is the **king termite**. **Worker termites** care for the queen's every need. They bring food, keep her clean and even clear up her droppings!

For many animals, eggs are juicy packets of food. But a predator might think twice about trying to steal eggs from a **bull ants'** nest. Worker bull ants are very fierce babysitters! They guard the eggs and grub-like babies, which are called larvae. The workers have large, strong, jaw-like mouthparts. They attack any intruder in the nest, biting them hard and squirting them with stinging acid.

Most insects are not very caring parents. The female lays the eggs, then leaves them. She does not look after them. Insect males usually do even less. The **giant water bug** of North America is an exception. The female glues her eggs to the male's folded wings. He keeps them out of danger until the eggs hatch.

Most female insects, such as this **window-winged moth**, lay lots of eggs. But they do not usually lay them just anywhere. Some, such as the female cockroach, choose a crack or crevice, where the eggs are hidden, protected and safe. The female window-winged moth sticks her eggs to a blade of grass – because that's what the baby caterpillars will eat. The caterpillars hatch out on to their food, and start to munch, straight away!

21

Live in groups?

Many, although not all bugs live in groups. The ones that do, find living together helps them to survive. Insects that live with others of their kind are called social insects. The main types are bees, wasps, ants and termites. They work together and help each other to find food and shelter, avoid danger and fight enemies. Some bugs seem to live in groups, but they have gathered together for other reasons. This may be at a food source, or in a safe place. These bugs will soon go their separate ways.

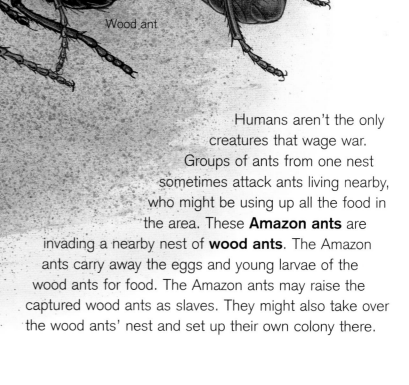

Amazon ant

Wood ant

Wood ant larva

Humans aren't the only creatures that wage war. Groups of ants from one nest sometimes attack ants living nearby, who might be using up all the food in the area. These **Amazon ants** are invading a nearby nest of **wood ants**. The Amazon ants carry away the eggs and young larvae of the wood ants for food. The Amazon ants may raise the captured wood ants as slaves. They might also take over the wood ants' nest and set up their own colony there.

Honeybees are social insects. They make honey – not for us, but for themselves. It is food for the worker bees. Workers look after the hive, gather flower nectar and other food, raise the young (larvae) and tend the queen. The queen lays the eggs. She eats a special type of honey, as do the growing bee larvae. A commercial beehive is designed so a beekeeper can lift out the combs and take out the honey easily.

Not all kinds of bees and wasps live in huge nests. Other kinds, such as the **potter wasp**, live alone and make small nests for their young. The female potter wasp shapes sand and mud, mixed with her saliva, to make a vase-shaped nest. She stings a caterpillar to paralyze it, and puts it inside for her larvae to eat when they hatch.

Woodlice are not really social insects. In fact, they aren't insects at all. They are crustaceans – land-dwelling relatives of crabs, shrimps and prawns. Woodlice gather together by chance because they need the same conditions to survive. They must stay in damp places, such as among old, rotting leaves or under moist, loose bark. If they get dry, they will die!

23

WHY DO BUGS...
Change shape?

As bugs grow up, their bodies change. This means that they can do different things at each stage of their life. Insects start as tiny eggs. The eggs then hatch into a second stage, the larva. This is the main feeding stage. Some larvae, such as butterfly caterpillars, look very different from the adults. They will change shape again to become full-grown adults. Other types of larvae, such as insect nymphs and baby spiders, look like their parents. They only change their shape slightly. They grow bigger until they, too, become adults.

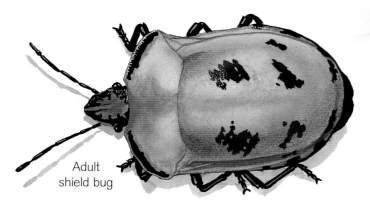

Adult
shield bug

A **shield bug** has a strong, hard body casing, like a knight's shield. The newly hatched young are called nymphs. They are similar to the parents, but their bodies are a slightly different shape and have no wings. They feed, grow and shed their skin several times. Each time they shed their skin, they look more like the adult.

Maggots squirm and writhe as they feed on rotting meat. Soon they will fly away. But how, without wings? Maggots and similar grubs are the larvae of flies such as the **greenbottle**. The soft-skinned larvae eat, shed their skin, wriggle, eat, shed their skin and so on. Then they change into tough-cased pupae. Inside the case, the fly forms its adult body. Finally it emerges and buzzes off!

Shield bug nymphs

24

These pictures show each stage in the life of an insect called a **swallowtail butterfly**. It begins as an egg. This hatches into the larva. In butterflies and moths, we call this a caterpillar. The larva sheds its skin several times as it grows. Then it becomes a hard-cased pupa, or chrysalis in the case of butterflies and moths. Inside the chrysalis, the body parts move around and change shape.

Egg

Young caterpillar (larva)

Older caterpillar (larva)

At last the adult emerges, crumpled and damp, from the chrysalis. The butterfly spreads its wings to dry, and then flits off to find a partner. This complete change in body shape is called metamorphosis. Other insects that go through these four different stages are moths, beetles, flies, bees, wasps and ants. Most other insects change shape gradually, from nymphs into the adults. This group includes shield bugs, grasshoppers, crickets, dragonflies and mayflies.

Adult butterfly

Chrysalis (pupa)

25

Live underwater?

Lots of animals, from worms and snails to tadpoles and fish, live underwater. They have all life's needs – food, shelter and breeding partners. For most bugs living underwater can be difficult, as they need to breathe air. They do not have special body parts, called gills, for breathing underwater. A bugs answer is to visit the surface regularly, for a supply of air. It stores this air as tiny bubbles around its body. Thousands of kinds of bugs live in ponds, streams, lakes and rivers – but none live in the sea.

The **great diving beetle** is the prime predator of the pond. This tiny terror attacks tadpoles, small fish and similar prey. It breathes air trapped under the hard, shiny wing cases on its back. It swims strongly by rowing with its oar-like legs. Like any other beetle, it can run on land with its legs and fly through the air with its wings.

Leeches are flattened relations of earthworms. Many live in water or damp places on land. They stick on to a larger creature, such as a fish or a horse, and suck out its blood and body fluids. The **medicinal leech** was used by doctors in medieval times to suck the blood from sick people. This was supposed to cure them, but often it made them even more ill!

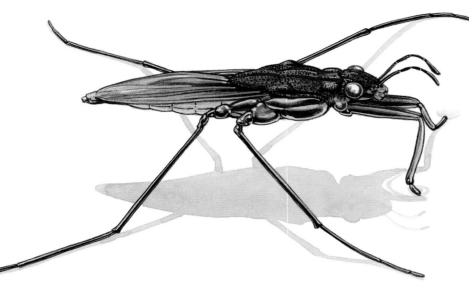

You can use a long tube called a snorkel to let you breathe air, while your face is underwater. The **water scorpion** has a kind of snorkel, too. But this breathing tube is on its tail, so its whole body can stay underwater! There is plenty of food in the water for the water scorpion. It hangs around in the weeds of a pond or lake. When a tadpole or similar prey passes by, the bug grabs it in its pincer-like front legs.

Some bugs live on the water instead of under it. The **pond skater** slides across the water's shiny surface, like a person skating on ice. Its tiny weight is held up by surface tension, which forms a 'thin skin' on top of the water. The pond skater slides over to tiny creatures trapped in the surface tension. Then the bug spears its prey with its sharp, needle-like mouthparts and sucks out the juices from the victim's body.

Like the water scorpion (above) this larva has a breathing tube on its tail. This larva is a maggot – when fully grown it will be a dronefly. Its 'snorkel' is so long that it looks like the tail of a rat. That is why it is called a **rat-tailed maggot**. Rat-tailed maggots love dirty, polluted water, just like rats!

Some water insects like the still conditions found in a pond or lake. In a fast stream, the current washes them away and crushes them. But not this **stonefly nymph**, the larva of the stonefly. It clings to the smooth pebbles on the stream bed with its strong, splayed-out legs and hook-like feet.

27

WHY DO BUGS...
Like people?

Usually because people provide them with food – though not willingly! A parasite is a creature that gets food, shelter and other needs from another animal, called a host. In the process, the parasite usually harms the host. For example, a parasite may suck blood from a host. Or a parasite might live in a host's gut. The gut is warm, moist and protected, with plenty of food for a parasite! Many parasites are small, and their hosts are big. Most bugs are small and we are big, so we are sometimes hosts to bug parasites. It's not only humans, but many other larger animals who get so close to bugs.

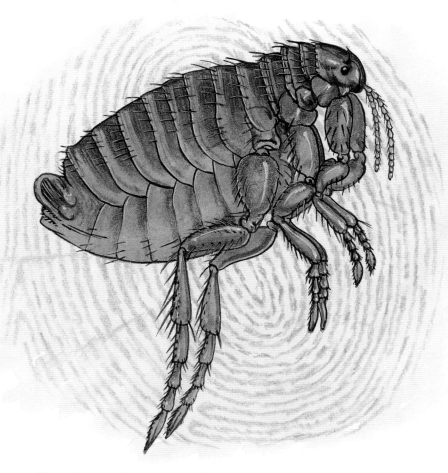

Meet the world champion long-jumper! Small as a pinhead, the **human flea** can leap up to 100 times its own body length! It has long, strong back legs for jumping, and it uses its hook-like middle and front legs to cling to its host's skin or hair. The flea's tall, thin body moves easily between the hairs. It pierces its host's skin with its sharp, spear-like mouth to suck its blood.

The **hard tick** lives on people and also on animals such as sheep and cattle. As it bites and sucks blood, it may spread germs and disease from one host to the next. Unlike the flea, this creature is not an insect. It's an arachnid – a tiny, eight-legged member of the spider group.

The **benchuca bug** has a long, needle-shaped 'beak'. Found in South America, this bug stabs its victim with its sharp mouthparts and sucks up its meal of blood. It does not drink enough blood to damage its victim, but it does carry tiny parasites in its gut that can cause harm. As the bug feeds, the tiny parasites can be transferred through the skin wound of its victim into their body. These 'germs' cause Chagas' disease – an illness that makes people feel weak and feverish.

Sleep tight and don't let the **bed bugs** bite! These bugs belong to a group of insects with long, tube-like snouts, which are used to suck up food. Bed bugs hide by day in cracks, crevices and bedding. At night, as we sleep, they crawl out to feed on our blood. Relatives of bed bugs don't have these vampire-like habits – they survive on plant sap.

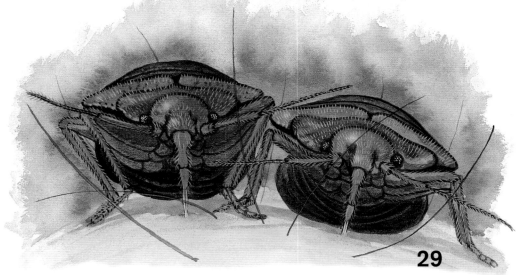

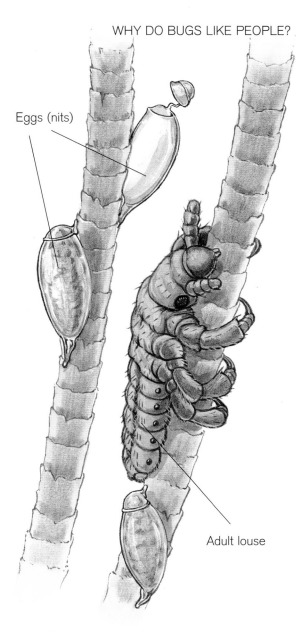

Eggs (nits)

Adult louse

The blood-sucking bites of **head lice** make the scalp itchy and sore. The louse's hook-shaped legs cling powerfully to hairs. Normal brushing or combing cannot remove it. The eggs, called nits, are glued to the hairs. They are even harder to remove. The best treatment is to wash the hair with a special anti-lice shampoo.

29

Like bugs?

People do like some bugs – most people think ladybirds or ladybugs are cute. But many insects and other creepy crawlies send shivers down our spine. Sometimes there's no good reason, because the creature is harmless. With others, though, we have good reasons to fear them. Some are pests, causing harm or damage. Others might bite, sting or poison us. Some bugs spread germs or illness. Others ruin our crops, plants and food. Bugs can also cause diseases in our animals. They burrow into wood and other substances in our houses, buildings and other structures. They even eat our clothes!

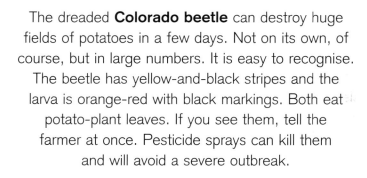

The dreaded **Colorado beetle** can destroy huge fields of potatoes in a few days. Not on its own, of course, but in large numbers. It is easy to recognise. The beetle has yellow-and-black stripes and the larva is orange-red with black markings. Both eat potato-plant leaves. If you see them, tell the farmer at once. Pesticide sprays can kill them and will avoid a severe outbreak.

Aaargh, help! It's a **tarantula**! Many people flee in fear. Others keep spiders as pets. Various big, hairy spiders are called tarantulas. But some have other, proper names, such as bird-eating spider. Tarantulas can give a powerful and painful bite, but they rarely kill people. Small spiders, such as the black widow of North America and the redback of Australia, are far more dangerous.

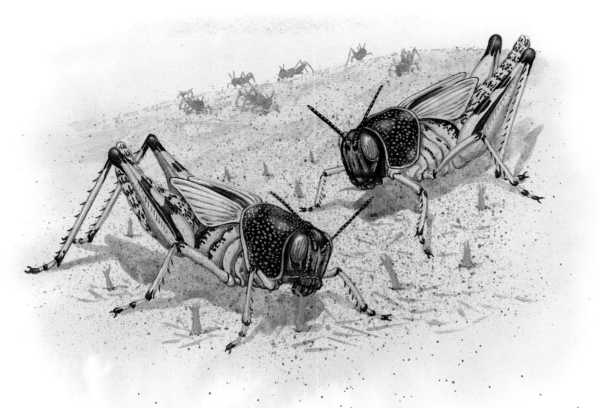

Every few years, huge swarms of **locusts** build up in areas of Africa and Asia. They fly long distances to find food. If they land on fields of farm crops, they can eat vast amounts in a day. Then they move on, breeding as they go. It's a disaster on a massive scale. Thousands of people go hungry or even starve. The young locust nymphs are called hoppers because their wings are small and they cannot fly. One way to kill locusts is by spraying pesticides from aircraft.

Some bugs cause harm by spreading deadly diseases. In Africa, the **tsetse fly** spreads a disease called nagana, or sleeping sickness. The fly bites an animal or a human – an ox, perhaps, which has the disease. It takes in the germs as it sucks up the blood. When the fly bites its next victim, it 'injects' the germs.

What has made the small holes in these gloves? It's the pesky **clothes moth**! Well, not the moth itself, but its caterpillars. The caterpillars change into pupae and then into adult moths, which lay eggs on the clothes again - its a never-ending circle!

31

Why are bugs so successful?

Insects, spiders and other bugs live all over the world. They are found in almost every habitat – from mountain-tops to forests, grasslands, deserts, lakes and rivers. Why are they so widespread and numerous? Bugs are small, so they don't need much food. They grow into adults quickly, so they can breed fast. Most have wings, so they can travel long distances. Some hide by camouflage. Others defend themselves by bites and stings. But most produce massive numbers of offspring, which secures their survival. Like them or loathe them – bugs are successful.

Index